I0426665

The History & Genealogy of the
Revey Family
of Monmouth County, New Jersey

Dr. Guadalupe Vanderhorst Rodríguez, D.Ac

Book Serenity

www.bookserenity.com

Please direct all correspondence and book orders to the following email address:

Book Serenity

www.bookserenity.com

Email: info@bookserenity.com

Or call 518.348.6200

Printed in the United States of America

ISBN: 978-1-304-59136-4

Dedication

Dedicated with heartfelt gratitude to the entire Revey family, with special appreciation extended to Tony Reevey for maintaining constant connection and Deborah Reevey for generously sharing her cherished family photographs.

This book is also devoted to the enduring legacy of my great-great-grandparents, Benjamin, and Mary E. (Nickens) Revey, whose footsteps paved the way for me to safeguard the rich history of the Revey family.

A profound tribute is paid to "Lone Bear" Revey, whose unwavering passion has kept us tethered to our indigenous heritage.

Lastly, this dedication extends to my beloved children, Kasennisaks, Kairhoktha, and Teiohonwake, and to my cherished grandchildren, Emilio, Valerie, Robert, Konner, Karma, and Eagle.

Table of Contents

Preface

In the year 1980, my journey into unraveling the intricate tapestry of my Monmouth County, New Jersey ancestors commenced. The focal point of my exploration was my great-grandfather, David S. Livingston. The impetus for this genealogical pursuit stemmed from the vivid memories shared by my grandmother, who frequently spoke of her father, David, and carried a locket containing his image. According to her narrative, he met a tragic end, having been mistaken for a deer and fatally shot. The Livingstons, it was revealed, hailed from Eatontown, New Jersey.

Eager to delve into the roots of my family tree, I embarked on a weekend trip to New Jersey, where I visited Beattie, my grandmother's first cousin. Beattie resided on Mechanic Street in Red Bank, New Jersey, conveniently located next door to her brother, Leonard Smith, and his wife, Marion. The proximity of family members was a recurring theme, reinforcing the tight-knit bonds within the families of Monmouth County New Jersey. Nestled in Bettie's living room, she unveiled the family bible, a repository of ancestral information. Turning to the page meticulously inscribed by my great-grandmother, Susan Rebecca (Johnson) Holmes, I stumbled upon the last entry – my grandmother, listed as Susan's youngest child.

The revelation that my grandmother's last name was Holmes, contrary to the longstanding belief that it was Livingston, prompted me to seek clarification from her directly. However, her response was shrouded in silence. Determined to unravel this mystery, I sought a copy of her birth record. To my surprise, the birth certificate, filed in 1954, confirmed her surname as "Holmes," along with the names of her parents. This unexpected twist redirected my focus, compelling me to delve into the labyrinth of the Holmes lineage.

Despite the initial divergence, my passion for genealogy remained steadfast, leading me to explore the Livingston family further. The breakthrough came with the discovery of the marriage certificate of Louis Livingston and Andrina Revey. Not only did this document solidify the familial connection, but it also provided the maiden names of the mothers – Sylvester and Nickens. This revelation opened new avenues for genealogical exploration, promising a richer understanding of my ancestral heritage.

As any seasoned genealogist knows, surnames often undergo variations for various reasons. Spelling discrepancies may arise due to the transcriber's unfamiliarity with the name or a deliberate choice by a family member to distinguish themselves. The Revey family name, for instance, traversed a linguistic journey throughout history, manifesting as Reve, Revy, Reavy, Revey, Reavey, Reevy, and Reevey. Notably, the descendants of Benjamin Reevey maintained the consistent spelling of "Reevey," while my ancestor, Benjamin Revey, and Mary E. Nickens adhered to the spelling "Revey." Despite these nuances, all emanated from the same ancestral lineage, tracing their roots back to Benjamin and Catherine (Runyon) Revy.

This juncture marked the inception of my exploration into the Revey family of Monmouth County, New Jersey. Motivated by a desire to preserve and share this rich genealogical tapestry, I resolved to document my findings in the form of a book. Through meticulous research and an unwavering commitment to unveiling the past, I endeavored to immortalize the branches of the Revey family tree.

In delving into the history of the Revey family, the nuances of spelling variations emerged as a recurring theme. The evolution of the surname from Reve to Reevey, coupled with the distinctive choices made by different branches, reflected the fluidity and adaptability of names across generations. Understanding the reasons behind these variations became a crucial aspect of my genealogical journey, shedding light on the individual choices and historical factors that contributed to the diversity in spellings.

One notable example was the Revey family's enduring commitment to maintaining the spelling "Reevey." Benjamin Reevey's descendants staunchly adhered to this specific iteration, creating a consistent thread through successive generations. In contrast, my own lineage, descending from Benjamin Revey and Mary E. Nickens, embraced the spelling "Revey." Despite the subtle differences, the shared ancestry underscored the unity within the Revey family, emphasizing the common roots that transcended linguistic variations.

As my research unfolded, I unearthed a trove of historical documents, each serving as a piece of the intricate puzzle that was the Revey family history. Marriage certificates, birth records, and family bibles became invaluable resources, allowing me to trace lineages, connect generations, and paint a vivid picture of the lives led by my ancestors in Monmouth County, New Jersey.

The marriage certificate of Louis Livingston and Andrina Revey emerged as a pivotal document. Beyond cementing the union of two individuals, it provided a gateway to the past by unveiling the names of their respective parents – Sylvester and Nickens. Armed with this newfound information, I embarked on a quest to expand the branches of my family tree, tracing the maternal lines and seeking to understand the stories embedded in each name.

The significance of maiden names extended beyond mere nomenclature; it became a key that unlocked doors to deeper genealogical exploration. The Sylvester and Nickens families, now integral parts of my ancestral tapestry, beckoned me to delve further into their histories. This unfolding journey offered not only a glimpse into the lives of these matriarchs but also an opportunity to connect with distant relatives and weave together a more comprehensive narrative of my family's past.

Navigating the labyrinth of genealogy necessitated an understanding of the fluid nature of surnames. The Revey family name, with its myriad spellings, exemplified this phenomenon, inviting contemplation of the factors that contributed to these linguistic variations. In the meticulous pursuit of historical accuracy, I encountered instances where names were altered due to transcription errors, linguistic evolution, or deliberate choices made by individuals to distinguish themselves from their familial counterparts.

The diverse spellings of the Revey surname were not anomalies but rather reflections of the dynamic nature of language and identity. Each iteration, whether Reve, Revy, Reavy, Revey, Reavey, Reevy, or Reevey, encapsulated a unique chapter in the family's journey. It became evident that the spelling of a surname was not a static entity, but a dynamic representation of the individual and collective choices made by each generation.

In chronicling the Revey family's history, my focus extended beyond the mere compilation of names and dates. It evolved into a quest to understand the motivations, challenges, and triumphs that shaped the lives of my ancestors. The Revey family, like any other, was a tapestry woven with threads of resilience, love, and the pursuit of a better future. Through the lens of genealogy, I sought to amplify these narratives, acknowledging the intricate stories embedded in the variations of the family surname.

Motivated by a deep sense of responsibility to preserve this rich heritage, I made the decision to share my findings with a broader audience. The culmination of my research materialized in the form of a book, a testament to the countless hours dedicated to unraveling the mysteries of the Revey family tree. It was not merely a collection of facts, but a narrative woven with the threads of familial bonds, historical contexts, and the resilience of the human spirit.

The process of writing this book became a journey of self-discovery, as I traversed through time,

INTRODUCTION

Within the pages of this book, you will embark on a captivating journey through the diverse branches of the Revey family. Our exploration commences with the early Revey family of Shrewsbury, New Jersey, unraveling the intricacies of their lives and relationships, including the revelation of the maiden names of their spouses. This compilation is a testament to the enduring legacy of the Revey family, meticulously crafted for the benefit of future generations.

Spanning over four generations, the narrative unfolds with a commitment to preserving the rich tapestry of the Revey family's history. Each page serves as a gateway to a bygone era, offering insights into the triumphs, challenges, and interconnected lives that have shaped the family's unique story. As we delve into the past, the aim is not just to unearth names and dates but to weave together a narrative that transcends generations, fostering a profound connection to our roots and fostering a sense of continuity for those yet to come.

This book begins with the early members of the Revey family, who are Benjamin Revey, his wife, Catherine Runyon, Joseph Revy, his wife Harriet, Abigail Revey, her spouse Edward Berry. The Revey descendants are described in their individual's section.

Also, the early documents for the Revey family have been transcribed for you.

To learn more about the Revey Family visit: www.reveyfamilyhistory.com

Monmouth County
New Jersey
History

Monmouth County is a county located in the state of New Jersey, United States. It was established on March 7, 1683, while part of the province of East Jersey [1]. The county was partitioned into the townships of Freehold, Middletown and Shrewsbury on October 31, 1693 [1]. The county seat is Freehold Borough [1].

If you are interested in learning more about the history of Monmouth County, I recommend checking out the book "History of Monmouth County, New Jersey" by Franklin Ellis and Norma Lippincott Swan [2]. This book provides a comprehensive overview of the county's history, including its early inhabitants, the Battle of Monmouth Court House during the American Revolution, and the county's establishment and development [2]. The book is available for free download at the Internet Archive website [2].

The name of Monmouth County has different historical theories. One theory is that the county was named after the Rhode Island Monmouth Society, which many of the county's earliest settlers originated from [12]. Another plausible theory is that the county was named after Monmouthshire in Wales, Great Britain, as suggested by Colonel Lewis Morris [12]. It is also possible that the county was named after James Scott, 1st Duke of Monmouth, who had many allies among the East Jersey leadership [12].

Monmouth County, located in the central part of New Jersey, has a rich and diverse history that spans centuries. The area was originally inhabited by indigenous peoples, primarily the Lenape, before European exploration and colonization. The history of Monmouth County is marked by significant events such as the Revolutionary War, industrialization, and suburban development.

INDIGENOUS PEOPLE IN NEW JERSEY

Before the arrival of Europeans, the Lenape Native Americans inhabited the region that would later become Monmouth County. They lived in small, semi-permanent villages, relying on hunting, fishing, and agriculture for sustenance. The Lenape had a profound connection to the land, and their culture was deeply rooted in the natural resources of the area.

The Lenape, also known as the Delaware Indians, are a Native American people who originally inhabited a vast region in the northeastern part of North America, including the area that is now Monmouth County, New Jersey. Their rich and complex culture was deeply intertwined with the natural environment, and their history spans thousands of years. Exploring the cultural aspects of the Lenape people in Monmouth County involves delving into their social structure, spiritual beliefs, daily life, and the impact of European colonization.

The Lenape were organized into loosely affiliated groups, each with its own leaders and governance structure. These groups were further divided into clans, with the Wolf, Turtle, and Turkey clans being among the most prominent. Clans played a crucial role in social organization, and individuals traced their lineage through their mother's clan. The Lenape were matrilineal, with women holding significant positions within the community and playing essential roles in decision-making.

Leadership within Lenape communities was often decentralized, with elders and sachems (leaders) guiding the group through consensus-based decision-making. These leaders were respected for their wisdom, experience, and ability to maintain harmony within the community.

The Lenape were skilled hunters, gatherers, and agriculturalists. They relied on the region's abundant natural resources for sustenance. Hunting provided them with games such as deer, elk, and smaller animals, while fishing in rivers and along the coast offered a variety of seafood.

Agriculture was also a crucial component of the Lenape economy. They cultivated crops such as maize (corn), beans, and squash, known as the "Three Sisters." This agricultural system was sustainable and enhanced soil fertility, showcasing Lenape's deep understanding of ecological balance.

The Lenape had a profound spiritual connection to the natural world, viewing the land, animals, and plants as sacred entities. Their belief system was animistic, attributing spirits to various elements of nature. These spirits were believed to influence daily life and were integral to the Lenape's spiritual practices.

The Lenape also had specific ceremonies and rituals to honor the seasons, express gratitude for the Earth's bounty, and seek guidance from the spiritual realm. The Green Corn Ceremony, for instance, celebrated the harvest and expressed gratitude for the sustenance provided by the land.

The Lenape language, a member of the Algonquian language family, was spoken by various Algonquian-speaking tribes in the region. The language was essential for communication within and between Lenape communities. Unfortunately, the Lenape language has largely disappeared, but efforts are ongoing to revitalize and preserve it.

Artistic expression among the Lenape included storytelling, oral traditions, and visual arts. Decorative beadwork, intricate baskets, and pottery were crafted with skill and precision. These art forms often conveyed spiritual or cultural significance, with designs representing aspects of Lenape life and beliefs.

WILLIAM PENN AND THE LENAPE

The arrival of European settlers, particularly the Dutch and English, had a profound impact on the Lenape way of life. Initial contact involved trade, with the Lenape exchanging furs, pelts, and other resources for European goods. However, as European colonization expanded, so did conflicts over land and resources.

The treaty signed between William Penn and the Lenape in 1682 is known as the Treaty of Shackamaxon[1]. It is also referred to as the Great Treaty or Penn's Treaty[1]. The treaty was signed under an ancient elm tree, which was later destroyed in a storm in 1810 [1]. The site of the treaty is now known as Penn Treaty Park[1]

However, the treaty was not honored by Penn's descendants, who began to encroach on Lenape land. This led to a series of disputes between the Lenape and the Penn family over land ownership[1].

Treaties were made and broken, leading to the forced relocation of Lenape communities. The Walking Purchase of 1737, a dubious land deal between the Penn family and the Lenape, resulted in the displacement of many Lenape from their ancestral lands in eastern Pennsylvania.

The Penns then hired runners to cover as much land as possible within a day and claimed that the land covered by the runners was part of the original deed. The Lenape were forced to cede the land to the Penns, which led to further disputes and violence[2].

In recent years, the Lenape have been fighting to reclaim their land and to have their history and culture recognized. In 2004, the Delaware Nation, one of three federally-recognized Lenape tribes, claimed 314 acres of land that was included in the Walking Purchase, but the claim was dismissed by the U.S. District Court[2]. The Lenape continue to advocate for their rights and to educate others about their history and culture[1]

Is European settlers continued to expand into Lenape territories, the Lenape faced increasing pressure and were eventually pushed westward. This displacement had devastating effects on their cultural practices, as they struggled to maintain their traditional way of life in the face of European encroachment.

Despite the challenges posed by European colonization, the Lenape people have persevered, and their cultural legacy endures. Efforts are underway to revitalize Lenape culture, language, and traditions. Tribal communities, cultural organizations, and scholars work to preserve and share the rich heritage of the Lenape people.

In Monmouth County and beyond, there is a growing acknowledgment of the historical and cultural significance of Lenape. Initiatives such as educational programs, museum exhibits, and collaborative projects with tribal communities contribute to a broader understanding of the Lenape's enduring legacy and the importance of preserving indigenous histories.

The Lenape people of Monmouth County, New Jersey, had a vibrant and interconnected culture deeply rooted in their relationship with the natural world. Their social structure, economic practices, spiritual beliefs, and artistic expressions reflected a profound connection to the land and a sustainable way of life. The impact of European colonization disrupted these centuries-old traditions, but contemporary efforts to preserve and revitalize Lenape culture contribute to a greater appreciation of their enduring legacy in the region.

Monmouth County was formally established on March 7, 1683, as one of New Jersey's original counties. On October 31, 1683, Monmouth County was partitioned into townships, Freehold, Middletown, and Shrewsbury.

COLONEL LEWIS MORRIS

Colonel Lewis Morris, aka "John Morris" was born in 1601, in Monmouthshire, Wales. He was a prominent figure in the early history of Monmouth County, New Jersey. He lived in Barbabos, West Indies. And later he became a successful entrepreneur and politician[12]. Morris is known for introducing slavery to Monmouth County by bringing enslaved workers from his sugar cane plantation in Barbados to provide bonded labor at his iron forge in Tinton Falls, New Jersey. Morris purchased a one-half interest in a bog iron property in Monmouth County near Colts Neck on December 29, 1675, and built an iron forge on the river in what today is Tinton Falls[1]. The burial ground for the enslaved people at this forge is located roughly at 741 Tinton Ave, Tinton Falls[1]. He owned land in the area called "Morrisana" in what is called the "Bronx".

The naming of Monmouth County has different historical theories. One theory is that the county was named after the Rhode Island Monmouth Society, which many of the county's earliest settlers originated from [12]. Another plausible theory is that the county was named after Monmouthshire in Wales, Great Britain, as suggested by Colonel Lewis Morris [12]. It is also possible that the county was named after James Scott, 1st Duke of Monmouth, who had many allies among the East Jersey leadership [12].

The region saw agricultural development, with farms and plantations becoming central to the local economy. During the 18th century, tensions between the American colonies and British authorities escalated, eventually leading to the American Revolution.

Monmouth County played a significant role in the Revolutionary War. The Battle of Monmouth, fought in June 1778, was a pivotal engagement between American and British forces. The Continental Army, led by General George Washington, clashed with British troops under General Sir Henry Clinton. The battle ended inconclusively, but it marked a turning point as it demonstrated the increasing capability of the Continental Army. The battlefield is now preserved as Monmouth Battlefield State Park, a testament to this critical moment in American history.

GROWTH OF MONMOUTH COUNTY, NEW JERSEY

In the 19th century, Monmouth County underwent significant changes with the rise of industrialization and transportation. The development of the railroad facilitated the movement of goods and people, spurring economic growth. Towns like Freehold and Red Bank saw increased industrial activity, including manufacturing and commerce. Agriculture remained a vital part of the economy, but the county also became a destination for summer resorts along the Jersey Shore.

During the Civil War, Monmouth County contributed men and resources to the Union cause. The war had a lasting impact on the region, with the post-war years witnessing efforts at reconstruction and the integration of formerly enslaved individuals into society.

The 20th century brought further changes to Monmouth County. The area experienced suburbanization, with population growth and the expansion of residential communities. Fort Monmouth, a significant military installation, played a crucial role during World War II and the Cold War. The county also became a hub for technology and research.

In recent decades, Monmouth County has continued to evolve. It remains a mix of suburban and rural landscapes, with a diverse economy that includes technology, healthcare, and education. The Jersey Shore, a popular destination for tourists, contributes significantly to the local economy.

Monmouth County's history is a tapestry woven with the threads of indigenous cultures, colonial struggles, industrialization, and suburban development. Its role in the Revolutionary War, the growth of agriculture and industry, and its transformation into a suburban landscape all contribute to the rich narrative of this central New Jersey County. As Monmouth County continues to embrace the future, its historical legacy serves as a foundation for understanding the dynamic forces that have shaped the region over the centuries.

REEVEYTOWN

Thomas Revey, lived in Shrewsbury, New Jersey during the early 1800's. It is believed Thomas was born about 1780. In 1804, Thomas Revey purchased land from Andrew Belle. And later, other Revey's purchased lands as well from Andrew Belle, in 1824, and 1827.

I partially transcribed this document was partially transcribed this document. It is the earliest record for the Revey family in Monmouth County, New Jersey that was discovered at the Monmouth County Clerk's office in Freehold, New Jersey.

'This indentured made the twenth day of October in the year of our Lord one thousand eight hundred and four, between Andrew Belle of Perth Amboy in the County of Middlesex and made of (?) of the one part, and Thomas Reevy of a place called horse ground on the Town of Shrewsbury in the County of Monmouth and State of New Jersey of said of the other part (?) that said Andrew Belle for and consideration of the sum of ninty two dollars and fifty cents to sum up known part by the ward Thomas C. Reey the (?) where of whereby acknowledge hath granted bargained and sold and by these

presents, Doth grant and bargain sell and release on (?) (?) (?) unto the said Thomas Reevy his heirs and a (?), (?) all that tract of land (?)
(?) in the Township of Shrewsbury in the County of Monmouth and division of the State of New Jersey. Beginning at the end of

four chains on a course south fourty degrees and nine (?) about (?) feel through formerly (?) on the south side with letters I.P. And now marked with the same- ward of shark (?) a place commonly called "the horse ground", which (?) is beginning corner of a triad of (?)and forty two hundred acre lot belonging to Joseph Poller, deceased and to Ann Knott Hunes running (I) East chain hence (2) South twentyone (?) chain........

REVEY FAMILY

REVEY FAMILY OF MONMOUTH COUNTY, NEW JERSEY

The Revey family of Monmouth County, New Jersey has deep roots in Shrewsbury, New Jersey. The earliest branch of the Revey family tree is found on a tax list in 1789 and the family is recorded in the 1830 Shrewsbury, New Jersey Census. These are the five branches of the Revey family tree.

These are the names in the Shrewsbury, New Jersey tax records in 1789:

Benjamin Reevy

Joseph Reevy

Thomas Reevy

William Reevy

William Reevy

REVEY FAMILY OF MONMOUTH COUNTY, NEW JERSEY

BENJAMIN REVEY

Benjamin Revey was born about 1770 in Monmouth County, New Jersey. On December 7, He married Catherine RUNYON on December 7, 1805, in Middlesex, New Jersey. Catherine Runyon was born about 1780.

Benjamin and Catherine (RUNYON) Revey's children:

Benjamin Revey was born about 1805 in Monmouth County, New Jersey. Bejamin Reevey married Mary Ann Revy, daughter of Joseph and Harriet Revy.

Richard Revey was born about 1814 in Monmouth County, New Jersey. Richard Revey married Nancy (Lydia).

Thomas Revey was born about 1817 in Monmouth County, New Jersey. Thomas D. Revey married Isabel.

Joseph Revey was born about 1818 in Monmouth County, New Jersey

James Revey was born about 1819 in Monmouth County, New Jersey.

Rebecca Revey was born about 1822 in Monmouth County, New Jersey.

Note: The years of birth are calculated on the ages according to the later census reports.

REVEY FAMILY OF MONMOUTH COUNTY, NEW JERSEY

Benjamin Revey

Benjamin Revey, son of Benjamin and Catherine RUNYON in Monmouth County, New Jersey. He married Mary Ann REVY on April 22, 1830, in Monmouth County, New Jersey. Mary Ann Revey, daughter of Joseph and Harriett Revey, possibly the brother of Benjamin Revey.

Benjamin and Mary Ann (REVY) REEVEY children:

Harriett Reevey, born 1828 in Monmouth County, New Jersey. On November 8, 1895, in Monmouth County, New Jersey Harriett died. She is buried at White Ridge Cemetery in Eatontown, New Jersey.

Rosanna Reevey was born 1831 in Monmouth County, New Jersey. In 1895, Rosanna Reevey lived in Neptune, New Jersey with Oscar Reevey, and Jane Reevey.

Joseph Reevey was born in 1833 in Monmouth County, New Jersey.

Thomas Reevey was born in 1835 in Monmouth County, New Jersey.

Margaret Reevey was born in 1841 in Monmouth County, New Jersey.

Benjamin Reevey (continued)

Catherine Reevey was born 1844 in Monmouth County, New Jersey. **Catherine A. Reevey** born 1872 in Monmouth County, New Jersey. She was the daughter of Benjamin and Mary Ann (REVY) REEVEY Catherine Revey married George ARMSTRONG. George was born Dec 1865 in Kentucky.

George and Catherine Armstrong's children:

Nathan Armstrong was born in 1888 in Monmouth County, New Jersey.

George A. Armstrong was born 1890 in Monmouth County, New Jersey.

Theresa Armstrong was born 1892 in Monmouth County, New Jersey.

Clarence Armstrong was born 1894 in Monmouth County, New Jersey.

Willanatta Armstrong was born 1896 in Monmouth County, New Jersey.

Eva Reevey born 1875 in Monmouth County, New Jersey. Eva Revey married George A. POLHEMUS on October 17, 1893, in Pine Book Monmouth County New Jersey.

Benjamin C. Reevey was born 1876 in Monmouth County, New Jersey. On April 29, 1897, in Fair Haven, New Jersey Benjamin C. Revey married Lenora BROWN

REVEY FAMILY OF MONMOUTH COUNTY, NEW JERSEY

Benjamin and Mary Ann (REVY) REEVEY children: (*continued*)

William Reevey was born 1846 in Monmouth County, New Jersey. **William Revey** was born 1846 in Monmouth County, New Jersey. His children were.

> **Serena Reevey**, born 1871 in Monmouth County, New Jersey. Serena Revey married Charles RICHARDSON. Serena Revey Richardson, died on July 1, 1965, buried at White Ridge Cemetery in Eatontown, New Jersey.

Charles Reevey was born 1847 in Monmouth County, New Jersey.

Richard Reevey was born 1850 in Monmouth County, New Jersey.

Jerusha Reevey

Cyrena Reevey

REVEY FAMILY OF MONMOUTH COUNTY, NEW JERSEY

Richard Revey

Richard Revey, son of Benjamin and Catherine Runyon in Monmouth County, New Jersey. Richard Revey married Nancy (Lydia), her maiden name is not known at this time.

Richard and Nancy (Lydia) Revey's children

> **Mary Revey** was born in 1838 in Monmouth County, New Jersey.

> **Thomas Revey** was born 1840 in Monmouth County, New Jersey.

> **Abigail Revey** was born in 1842 in Monmouth County, New Jersey.

> **Benjamin Revey** was born 1844 in Monmouth County, New Jersey. On November 30, 1867, in Monmouth County, New Jersey Benjamin Revey married Mary E. *NICKENS*, daughter of Hiram and Leta (*REVEY*) Nickens.

> **Margaret Revey** was born 1846 in Monmouth County, New Jersey.

Richard Revey (continued)

Rebecca Revey was born 1848 in Monmouth County, New Jersey. Rebecca Revey married Joseph WALL.

Joseph and Rebecca (Revey) Wall's children:

> **Florence Wall** was born in 1871 in Monmouth County, New Jersey.

> **Abigail (Abby) Wall** was born in 1874 in Monmouth County, New Jersey.

> **Samuel Wall** was born in 1878 in Monmouth County, New Jersey.

Charles Revey was born 1851 in Monmouth County, New Jersey. Charles Revey married Mary A. TAYLOR in Monmouth County, New Jersey.

Charles and Mary A. (TAYLOR) Revey's children:

> *Charles Edward Revey* was born in January 1876 in Monmouth County, New Jersey. Charles E. married Harriet.

> Charles and Harriett Revey's children:

> > *Ada L. Revey* was born 1911 in Monmouth County, New Jersey.

Charles Revey (continued)

Rev. Kingdom Joseph Revey was born on April 10, 1912, in Monmouth County, New Jersey, son of Charles and Harriett Revey. Kingdom J. Revey married Roberta HART, daughter of Joseph HART.

Kingdom and Roberta (HART) Revey's children:

Mary E. Revey was born 1937 in Monmouth County, New Jersey.

Alice Revey was born 1940 in Monmouth County, New Jersey. Alice Revey married Mr. Watts.

Eleanor Revey was born in 1940 in Monmouth County, New Jersey.

Rev. Kingdom Revey died in Charlotte, North Carolina on May 14, 1998.

Violet Revey was born 1918 in Monmouth County, New Jersey.

Olivia Revey was born 1920 in Monmouth County, New Jersey. Olivia Revey married Willam H. QUILL.

Richard Revey

Vianer Revey was born 1854 in Monmouth County, New Jersey, son of Richard and Nancy (Lydia).

Joseph Revey was born 1856 in Monmouth County, New Jersey, son of Richard and Nancy (Lydia).

REVEY FAMILY OF MONMOUTH COUNTY, NEW JERSEY

Thomas Revey, son of Benjamin and Catherine Runyon Revey in Monmouth County, New Jersey born in 1817. Thomas Revey married Isabel. Her maiden's name is not known. Isabel was born in 1826.

Thomas and Isabel Revey's children were:

> **Ebenezar Revey** was born 1847 in Monmouth County, New Jersey.
>
> **William Revey** was born 1850 in Monmouth County, New Jersey.
>
> **Richard Revey** was born in 1855 in Monmouth County, New Jersey.
>
> **Mary Revey** was born 1857 in Monmouth County, New Jersey.
>
> **Thomas D. Revey** was born about 1861 in Monmouth County, New Jersey. Thomas Revey married Lavina THOMPSON.
>
> **John Revey** was born 1861 in Monmouth County, New Jersey. John Revey married Sarah COY.

REVEY FAMILY OF MONMOUTH COUNTY, NEW JERSEY

Ebenezar Revy, was born in 1838 in Monmouth County, New Jersey. Ebenezer Revy is the son of Thomas and Isabel Revy. He married Ann *HOLMES*, born 1840 in Monmouth County, New Jersey, daughter of Slias Holmes of Monmouth County, New Jersey.

Ebenezar and Ann Revy children were:

> *Augustine Revy*, Revy born 1866 in Monmouth County, New Jersey. Augustine Revy, son of Ebenezar and Ann HOLMES Revy born 1866 in Monmouth County, New Jersey.

> **Monroe Revy** was born 1869 in Monmouth County, New Jersey.

> **Oscar Revy** was born July 1871 in Monmouth County, New Jersey. Oscar Revy spouse was Lucy.

> **Ebenezer Franklin Revy** was born November 16, 1877, in Monmouth County, New Jersey. Ebenezar Revy married Isabel.

REVEY FAMILY OF MONMOUTH COUNTY, NEW JERSEY

Augustine Reevey

> *Augustine Reevey* was born 1864 in Monmouth County, New Jersey. Augustine Reevey, son of Ebenezer and Ann (HOLMES) Reevey.
>
> *Augustine Reevey* was married to Ameilia. Ameila had a daughter, Mary E. Farrol born 1896.
>
> *Augustine and Amelia Reevey child:*
>
> > *Harold Leander Reevey* was born in 1910 in Monmouth County, New Jersey.
>
> **Augustine Reevey** married Dora Williams in Monmouth County, New Jersey. Dora Williams was born in Fayetteville, North Carolina. Augustine was a carpenter in New Jersey.
>
> Augustine and Dora (Williams) Reevey's children:
>
> > *Edward Reevey* was born 1911 in Monmouth County, New Jersey.
> >
> > *Frances Reevey* was born in 1914 in Monmouth County, New Jersey.
> >
> > *William Reevey* was born in 1919 in Monmouth County, New Jersey. William Reevey married Bertha.
> >
> > *Stanley Reevey* was born December 12, 1919 in Monmouth County, New Jersey. Stanley Reevey married Mamie L. DANIELS in March 1955 in Monmouth County, New Jersey.

Augustine Reevey (continued)

> **Ralph Henry Reevey** was born in 1921 in Monmouth County, New Jersey. Ralph H. Reevey married Beatrice SHIELDS.

> **Gertrude Reevey** was born in 1924 in New Jersey.

William Revey

> **William Revey** was born 1850 in Monmouth County, New Jersey, son of Thomas and Isabel Revey. William Revey married Rebecca RICHARDSON, born in 1859, daughter of Charles B and Maria RICHARDSON of Shrewsbury, New Jersey.

William and Rebecca (RICHARDSON) Revey's children:

> **Rebecca Revey** was born 1872 in Monmouth County, New Jersey. Rebecca Revey married George BOWLES in Monmouth County, New Jersey.

> George and Rebecca (REVEY) Bowles children:

> > **L. Grant Bowles** born in 1888 in Monmouth Co. NJ

> > **Edith M. Bowles** born in 1896 in Monmouth County, New Jersey. Edith Bowles married Mr. Taylor. Their children, Percy Taylor born 1918, and Edna Taylor born 1920.

> > **William M. Bowles** was born in 1907 in Monmouth County, New Jersey.

> > **David I. Bowles** born in Monmouth County, NJ

William Revey *(continued)*

George and Rebecca (REVEY) Bowles children: (continued)

Mary Elizabeth Bowles was born 1910 in Monmouth County, New Jersey. Mary Revey married Mr. Obie Clifford Day born 1910 in North Carolina.

Irita R. Bowles was born 1912 in Monmouth County, New Jersey.

John Bowles born in Monmouth County, NJ

William Revey

Charles Benjamin. Revey was born April 10, 1876, in Monmouth County, New Jersey.

Cassandra Revey was born 1896 in Monmouth County, New Jersey.

Martha Revey was born 1898 in Monmouth County, New Jersey.

REVEY FAMILY OF MONMOUTH COUNTY, NEW JERSEY

Richard Peter Revey

Richard Peter Revey, son of Thomas and Isabel Revey, was born 1855 in Monmouth County, New Jersey. Richard Revey married Rebecca E HOLMES.

Richard and Rebecca (HOLMES) Revey children:

> **(Richard) Nelson Revey**, born on March 24, 1878, in Monmouth County, New Jersey. In 1918 in Monmouth County, New Jersey Richard N. Revey married Mabel CHAPMAN.

> **Ralph Augustus. Revey** was born 1880 in Monmouth County, New Jersey.

REVEY FAMILY OF MONMOUTH COUNTY, NEW JERSEY

Mary Revey

> **Mary Revey**, born 1857 in Monmouth County, New Jersey, daughter of Thomas and Isabel Revey.

REVEY FAMILY OF MONMOUTH COUNTY, NEW JERSEY

Thomas D. Revey

Thomas D. Revey, son of Thomas and Isabel Revey, was born in January 1861 in Monmouth County, New Jersey. Thomas Revey married Lavina THOMPSON.

Thomas and Lavinia (Thompson) Revey's children:

> **Isabelle Reevey**, born 1880, in Monmouth County, New Jersey.

> **Mary E. Reevey**, born 1882, in Monmouth County, New Jersey.

> **Charlotte Reevey**, born 1887, in Monmouth County, New Jersey.

> **Florence Reevey**, born 1889, in Monmouth County, New Jersey.

> **Laura V. Reevey**, born 1893 in Monmouth County, New Jersey.

> **Martha Reevey** was born 1901 in Monmouth County, New Jersey.

> **Eleanore Reevey** was born 1909 in Monmouth County, New Jersey.

REVEY FAMILY OF MONMOUTH COUNTY, NEW JERSEY

Richard Revey

Richard Revey, born 1850 in Monmouth County, New Jersey. Richard REEVEY was the son of Benjamin and Mary Ann (REVY) REEVEY. Richard P. Revey married Esther F. VINCENT or Rebecca E. HOLMES.

> *Charles Reavy*, son of Benjamin and Mary Ann Revy, was born in 1847 in Monmouth County, New Jersey. The grandson of Benjamin & Catherine (Runyon) Reve. Charles Reavy married Hagar A. SPENCER, born On December 31, 1879 in the Town of Shrewsbury, NJ Charles Reavy married Hagar A. *SPENCER*, born 1859, daughter of Robert (b.1822) and Caroline Spencer (b. 1826) in Monmouth County, New Jersey.

> > **Elizabeth F. Reavy** was born 1871 in Monmouth County, New Jersey.

> > *Hagar Spencer* **Reavy** was born. She died on May 27, 1894 in Shrewsbury, New Jersey.

REVEY FAMILY OF MONMOUTH COUNTY, NEW JERSEY

RICHARD & NANCY (Lydia)REVEY

Richard, Revey, son of Benjamin and Catherine Runyon in Monmouth County, New Jersey. He married Nancy, her surname is not known at this time. Richard and Nancy (Lydia) Revey's children:

> *Mary Revey* born 1838 in Monmouth County, New Jersey.
>
> *Thomas Revey* born 1840 in Monmouth County, New Jersey
>
> *Abigail Revey* born 1842 in Monmouth County, New Jersey
>
> *Benjamin Revey* was born 1844 in Monmouth County, New Jersey. Benjamin Revey married Mary E. Nickens. Mary E. Nickens, daughter of Hiram Nickens and Leta REVEY.
>
> *Margaret Revey* born 1846 in Monmouth County, New Jersey
>
> *Rebecca Revey born 1848* in Monmouth County, New Jersey

REVEY FAMILY OF MONMOUTH COUNTY, NEW JERSEY

RICHARD & NANCY (Lydia) REVEY

Charles Revey was born 1851 in Monmouth County, New Jersey. Charles Revey married Mary A. TAYLOR in Monmouth County, New Jersey.

Charles and Mary A. (TAYLOR) Revey's children:

Charles Edward Revey was born in January 1876 in Monmouth County, New Jersey. Charles E. married Harriet, and their children:

Ada L. Revey born 1911 in Monmouth County, New Jersey.

Kingdom Revey was born 1915 in Monmouth County, New Jersey.

Violet Revey was born 1918 in Monmouth County, New Jersey.

Olivia Revey was born 1920 in Monmouth County, New Jersey. Olivia Revey married Willam H. QUILL.

Vianer Revey was born 1854 in Monmouth County, New Jersey.

REVEY FAMILY OF MONMOUTH COUNTY, NEW JERSEY

Joseph Revey

Joseph Revey was born 1856, son of Richard and Nancy Revey in Monmouth County, New Jersey. He is the grandson of Benjamin and Catherine (Runyon) Revey.

Joseph married Lucinda (Revey), born 1869, daughter of William Revey.

Joseph and Lucinda Revey's stepdaughter, Harriett (Revey) Taylor, born 1897 in Shrewsbury, NJ.

> **Harriett Revey** married Mr. Taylor and their children:
>
> > **Evelyn Taylor**, born 1914 in Monmouth County, New Jersey.
> >
> > **Dorothy Taylor**, born 1915 in Monmouth County, New Jersey.
> >
> > **Bernice Taylor** was born 1916 in Monmouth County, New Jersey.

REVEY FAMILY OF MONMOUTH COUNTY, NEW JERSEY

Benjamin Revey

Benjamin Revey, son of Richard and Nancy Revey, and grandson of Benjamin and Catherine (Runyon) Revey. Benjamin Revey was born in 1835 in Eatontown, New Jersey. On November 16, 1867, he married Mary Elise Nickens, born 1858, daughter of Hiram and Leta Nickens. Hiram Nickens was born in 1790, possibly in Maryland. He enlisted in the Military. And Hiram and Leta (b. 1822) lived in New York City. Hiram and Leta Nickens had three children, Hiram Nickens, Mary Elise Nickens, and Julia Nickens.

Benjamin and Mary Revey had six children,

Andrina Revey was born 1867 in Monmouth County, New Jersey. Andrina Revey married Louis Livingston, son of George and Sarah Jane (SYLVESTER) Livingston. Louis and Andrina (REVEY) Livingstons children were:

Phineas Revey, born 1869 in Monmouth County, New Jersey.

Catherine Revey, born 1872 in Monmouth County, New Jersey. Catherine Revey married John RICHARDSON.

Wilmeta Revey born 1874 in Monmouth County, New Jersey. May have had a daughter born on February 18, 1889 in Monmouth County, New Jersey. Williametta Revey died on June 13, 1894, in Monmouth County, New Jersey.

Benjamin Revey (*continued*)

Charles S. Revey, born 1876 in Monmouth County, New Jersey **Charles S. Revey** was born in 1876 in Monmouth County, New Jersey. Charles S. Revey married Laura V.

Bloomfield Revey, born 1878 in Monmouth County, New Jersey. In 1904, Bloomfield Revey married Fannie Van Brockle in Monmouth County, New Jersey. Fannie Vanbrocke was the granddaughter of Isaiah and Margaret (Dwight) Revy and Georgianne Thorton.

REVEY FAMILY OF MONMOUTH COUNTY, NEW JERSEY

Andrina Revey

Andrina Revey, married Louis Livingston, born 1862, son of George and (Sarah)Jane (SYLVESTER) Livingston, Andrina and Louis and lived in Eatontown, New Jersey with their five children.,

> **Stanley Livingston** was born in May 1885 in Monmouth County, New Jersey.
>
> **Bessie Livingston** was born in 1886 in Monmouth County, New Jersey.
>
> **David Sylvester Livingston** was born October in 1889 in Monmouth County, New Jersey.
>
> **Lloyd Livingston** was born in 1892 in Monmouth County, New Jersey.
>
> **Viola Livingston** was born September 1897 in Monmouth County, New Jersey.

Andrina Revey (continued)

Stanley Livingston, married Ida Lockwood, daughter of Joseph and Elizabeth (Grinrod) Lockwood. Stanley and Ida Livingston had one son, Stanley Livingston jr, born 1907 and died   and infant. They are buried at White Ridge Cemetery in Eatontown, New Jersey.

Stanley Livington Jr. born 1907-1907, son of Stanley and Ida Livingston. Stanley is buried at White Ridge Cemetery in Eatontown, New Jersey.

Bessie Livington, born February 1887 in Eatontown, New Jersey, daughter of Louis and Andrina (REVEY) Livingston. In 1907, Bessie Livingston married George TERRY in Monmouth County, New Jersey.

George & Bessie (LIVINGSTON) Terry's children were:

> **Mildred Terry**, born 1910 in Monmouth County, New Jersey,

> **Louis Terry**, was born 1911 in Monmouth County, New Jersey.

> **Gladys Terry** was born 1912 in Monmouth County, New Jersey.

> **Raymond Terry** was born in 1914 in Monmouth County, New Jersey.

> **Helen Terry** was born in 1916 in Monmouth County, New Jersey

ANDRINA REVEY *(continued)*

BESSIE LIVINGTON, born February 1887 in Eatontown, New Jersey, daughter of Louis and Andrina (REVEY) Livingston. Bessie Livingston is buried in White Ridge Cemetery, New Jersey.

In 1907, Bessie Livingston married George TERRY in Monmouth County, New Jersey. Bessie and George Terry's children were

Mildred Terry, born 1910 in Monmouth County, New Jersey,

Louis Terry, was born 1911 in Monmouth County, New Jersey.

Gladys Terry was born 1912 in Monmouth County, New Jersey.

Raymond Terry was born 1914 in Monmouth County, New Jersey.

Helen Terry was born 1916 in Monmouth County, New Jersey.

Note: There is a child, John James Terry born to George and Bessie (Livingston), the year is unknown. Bessie (Livingston) Terry is buried at White Ridge Cemetery in Eatontown, New Jersey.

ANDRINA REVEY *(continued)*

> **DAVID SYLVESTER LIVINGSTON**, born 1889 in Monmouth County, New Jersey. David Livingston, and Maude *HOLMES*, had a daughter, Dorothy Mae Livingston/Holmes.
>
> David Livingston died of a gun shot on February 17, 1910, in Red Bank, New Jersey. David is buried at White Ridge Cemetery in Eatontown, New Jersey.
>
> **LLOYD LIVINGSTON**
>
> **VIOLA LIVINGSTON,** married Daniel TERRY and lived in Red Bank, New Jersey. Viola (*Livington*) Terry died on October 7, 1958, in Eatontown, New Jersey. She is buried at White Ridge Cemetery Eatontown, New Jersey.

REVEY FAMILY OF MONMOUTH COUNTY, NEW JERSEY

DAVID SYLVESTER LIVINGSTON

David S. Livingston was born in October 1889, in Eatontown, New Jersey. The son of Louis Livingston and Andrina (Revey) Livingston.

On the night of February 17, 1910, in Red Bank, New Jersey, an unfortunate incident unfolded in the history of the Revey family. David, accompanied by his friends Robert Mountjoy and Tom Seward, spent the evening exploring the 'saloons' of Red Bank while the local police were engrossed in their annual ball, attended by many officers from the community.

As the trio strolled beneath the moonlit sky, Rob and David, arm in arm, discharged their pistols into the air. Unbeknownst to Rob, as he casually pocketed his firearm, a shot rang out, striking David in the side. Collapsing to the ground, David's final words were a plea to inform his mother, "Tell, Mama, I've been shot. "His last words for the unfortunate incident, blood escaping from his mouth. Doubtful, Rob dismissed it as a jest, urging David to cease his playful antics.

In a panic, Tom Seward rushed to the Livingston home, where Louis Livingston arrived to find his son lying lifeless in the street. Despite the tragic circumstance, Louis addressed Rob with remarkable calmness, stating, "You were like a brother to Dave." This chilling event remains etched in the annals of the Revey family history.

REVEY FAMILY OF MONMOUTH COUNTY, NEW JERSEY

David Sylvester Livingston

This is an excerpt from Rob Mountjoy's Trial:

Testimony by Thomas Seward about the death of David Livingston:

Q: What was Monjoy doing?

A: Rob was revolving his gun,

Q: Do you mean pulling the Trigger?

A: Yes, sir snapping it, He snapped it every about four times before it fired. Rob says, "I have no more balls in my gun". So he kept firing, kept firing bout four times. And about the fifth time it shot and shot David in the shoulder. . So then Dave said, "Rob, you have shot me." Rob says, "Oh, Dave you are fooling." Dave says, " Oh, yes, you have shot me." Rob says, Oh, Dave you know I haven't shot you. Where have I shot you?" He said, " You have shot me in my back, Like that and Rob commenced to find out whether it was so, I don't know so Dave siay, Rob you have shot me. He says, "Tell Mama, I am shot, I am shot". He did not live but three minutes after he was shot.

Tom Seward ran to the Livingston home to get Dave's father, Louis. When Louis arrived to where his son's body laid, Louis Livingston looked at Rob Mountjoy and said, *"Dave was like a brother to you"*.

David S. Livingston was shot on February 17, 1910 in Red Bank, New Jersey by Rob Mountjoy.

David Sylvester Livingston

REVEY FAMILY OF MONMOUTH COUNTY, NEW JERSEY

Benjamin Revey and Catherine (RUNYON) Revey

James Revey and Lucinda

Johnson B. Revey and Restelle (RICHARDSON) Revey. Johnson Benjamin Revey was born in 1864 in Monmouth County, New Jersey, son of James and Lucinda Revey.) On October 19, 1893, in Asbury Park, New Jesey, Johnson Revey married Restelle Richardson.

Johnson and Restelle (RICHARDSON) Revey's children were:

James R. Revey (b. 1895)

Robert V. Revey was born 1897 in Monmouth County, New Jersey. Robert V. Revey married Vivian RITTER.

Mercedes Revey was born in 1922.

James "Lone Bear" Revey was born in January 29, 1924 in Monmouth County, New Jersey. He died on May 18, 1998, in East Orange, New Jersey.

In 1950, the Revey family lived on Vine Street in Lynbrook, Nassau County New York. Robert Revey 53 years old was employed as a manager for a trucking company, His wife, Vivian Revey was 50 years old, and their son James Revey was employed as an *Indian Craft Maker*. Also, living in the household was Charlotte Younger, Vivian's mother. In 1940, the Revey family on E163 street lived in the Bronx.

Other Branches
of the
Revey Family Tree

Other Branches of the Revey Family Tree

The Revey Family Tree, like many others, extends its branches to encompass a diverse array of descendants. However, tracing the connections among these branches poses a formidable challenge due to the limitations of historical documents, particularly the U.S. Census and other primary sources. Unraveling the ancestral threads that bind various segments of the Revey family proves to be a complex task, hindered by the inherent gaps and inaccuracies within these records.

The vast tapestry of the Revey Family Tree bears witnesses to the passage of time and the emergence of numerous offshoots, each representing a unique lineage within the larger family framework. Despite the shared heritage, the connections between these branches remain elusive, shrouded in the obscurity of incomplete or unreliable documentation. This predicament is particularly evident when attempting to delve into the distant past and uncover the identities of the forebears who laid the foundations for the diverse Revey family descendants we see today.

A central obstacle in the quest for accurate genealogical information is the inherent limitations of historical records, with the U.S. Census standing out as a primary source of contention. While the census has been a crucial tool for documenting demographic shifts and familial structures, its reliability diminishes when applied to tracing specific familial lineages. Incomplete or missing data, variations in name spellings, and the subjective nature of responses contribute to the challenges faced by genealogists seeking to piece together the intricate puzzle of the Revey family's history.

The U.S. Census, a cornerstone of genealogical research, is conducted decennially, providing snapshots of the population at different points in time. However, these snapshots are not without their flaws. Inconsistencies in data collection methods, transcription errors, and the voluntary nature of certain census years contribute to the gaps in the historical record. Consequently,

Other Branches of the Revey Family Tree

the Revey Family Tree, like many others, grapples with the consequences of these limitations as it endeavors to trace the intricate web of familial connections.

Beyond the U.S. Census, other primary sources present similar challenges. Birth and death certificates, marriage records, and immigration documents, while valuable, are not immune to inaccuracies. The reliability of these sources' hinges on factors such as the diligence of record-keepers, the accuracy of information provided by individuals, and the preservation of documents over time. In the case of the Revey family, these factors add layers of complexity to the pursuit of a comprehensive and accurate family history.

The absence of a centralized repository for genealogical information further compounds the difficulties faced by those seeking to explore the Revey Family Tree. Unlike more recent generations, where digitization and online databases facilitate access to a wealth of information, tracing ancestral roots becomes a laborious task when dealing with historical records that may be scattered across different archives, libraries, or even private collections. This decentralized nature of genealogical information poses a formidable hurdle for those attempting to weave together the disparate strands of the Revey family's past.

Despite these challenges, the quest to unravel the Revey Family Tree's mysteries persists, fueled by the dedication of genealogists and family historians. Collaborative efforts, supported by advancements in technology and the digitization of records, offer glimmers of hope in overcoming the hurdles posed by incomplete or elusive primary sources. DNA testing has emerged as a powerful tool, allowing individuals to establish genetic connections and bridge the gaps left by the limitations of traditional genealogical research.

Other Branches of the Revey Family Tree

The Revey family's journey through time and across generations is a testament to the resilience of familial ties. While the challenges in reconstructing the family tree are undeniable, the pursuit of this knowledge holds immeasurable value for descendants seeking a deeper understanding of their roots. It is a journey that requires patience, meticulous research, and a willingness to embrace the uncertainties inherent in the exploration of historical records.

In navigating the complexities of the Revey Family Tree it becomes evident that the quest for ancestral knowledge extends beyond the confines of conventional genealogical research. Oral histories, passed down through generations, become invaluable in filling the gaps left by official records. Family stories, anecdotes, and traditions offer a richer tapestry of the Revey family's narrative, providing a more nuanced understanding of the lives and experiences of its diverse members.

The Revey Family Tree, with its enigmatic branches, serves as a microcosm of the broader challenges faced by genealogists and family historians. As society evolves and historical records become increasingly digitized, opportunities for uncovering hidden connections within the family tree multiply. The Revey family's story is an ongoing saga, where each generation contributes to the ever-expanding narrative, adding layers of complexity and richness to the family's collective history.

In conclusion, the Revey Family Tree stands as a testament to the intricacies inherent in tracing ancestral roots, especially when confronted with the limitations of historical documents like the U.S. Census and other primary sources. The challenges faced in connecting various branches underscore the need for innovative approaches, collaborative efforts, and a holistic understanding of genealogical research. As technology and methodologies continue to advance, the Revey family, like others, has the potential to unlock new chapters in its history, bringing to light the stories of ancestors who have long remained hidden in the shadows of time. The pursuit of the Revey Family Tree's complete story is a journey that transcends generations, bridging the past with the present and illuminating the path for future descendants eager to explore their familial heritage.

Other Branches of the Revey Family Tree

Ann REEVEY

Ann Reevey, was born in 1784 in Monmouth County, New Jersey. Ann Reevey married Andrew Richardson in Monmouth County, New Jersey.

ABIGAIL REVY

Abigail Revy, born about 1800, parents unknown. Abigail Revy married Samuel Dwight on December 16, 1826 in Monmouth County, New Jersey.

ABIGAIL REVEY

Abigail Revey married Aron Lee on January 27, 1827, in Monmouth County, New Jersey.

FREDERICK REEVY

Frederick Reevy born 1873, in Monmouth County, New Jersey. His parents are not known currently. Frederick Reevy married Josephine in 1892 in Monmouth County, New Jersey. Their children

> **Helen C. Revey**, born June 1892 in Monmouth County, New Jersey
>
> **Isadore M. Revey**, born 1895 in Monmouth County, New Jersey.

Other Branches of the Revey Family Tree

ELIZA REVY

Eliza Revy was born about 1830 in Monmouth County, New Jersey. Her parents are not known. On December 30, 1852, in Monmouth County, New Jersey, Harriett aka Eliza Revy married Johnson Vancleaf. Johnson Vancleaf was born in 1818 in Monmouth County, New Jersey. Johnson and Eliza (Revy) Vancleaf's children:

> **Elmira Vancleaf**
>
> **Eugene Vancleaf**
>
> **William H. Vancleaf**
>
> **Elijah Vancleaf**

JOHN REEVY- Marriage

On January 8, 1884, in Fair Haven, Monmouth County, New Jersey, John Reevey married Sadie COY.

ISSIAH REVEY

Issiah Revy, born married Margaret DWIGHT they lived in Monmouth County, New Jersey.

> **Emeline Revy** born 1850 in Monmouth County, New Jersey. Emeline Revy married George Vanbrockle. Their children were Fannie Vanbrockle, and George Vanbrockle. Fannie Vanbrockle, is the granddaughter of Issac and Margaret Revy. Fannie married Bloomfield Revey, son of Benjamin and Mary E. (Nickens) Revey.

Other Branches of the Revey Family Tree

ISIAH REVEY

Samuel Revy born July 1853 in Shrewsbury, Monmouth County, New Jersey. Samuel Reevey married Lottie. Lottie was born in October 1866 in Maryland.

Samuel and Lottie Catherine Reevey's children:

Mable Revey born August 1883 in Monmouth County, New Jersey

Orlean Revy was born 1855 in Monmouth County, New Jersey.

Deborah Revy, born 1857 in Monmouth County, New Jersey. On January 19, 1880, in Monmouth County, New Jersey, she died at the age of 23.

David Revy, born 1859 in Monmouth County, Jersey.

Horace Revy was born 1868 in Monmouth County, new Jersey.

Lucinda Revy was born 1865 in Monmouth County, New Jersey.

James Revey was born 1867 in Monmouth County, New Jersey.

Rodney Revey was born In 1870 in Monmouth County, New Jersey.

Other Branches of the Revey Family Tree

ISIAH REVEY

Samuel and Lottie Catherine Reevey's children: (continued)

Norman L. Reevey born March 1893 in Monmouth County, New Jersey. Norman Reevey was married to Beulah.

Samuel H. Reevey born April 1896 in Monmouth County New Jersey.

Hosea Reevey born July 1898 in Monmouth County New Jersey. Hosea Frances Reevey married Fannie ARCHER daughter of Daniel and Mary Louise Archer.

Hosea and Fannie (Archer) Reevey's children were.

Milton Reevey born 1924 Monmouth County New Jersey

Norma Reevey, born 1926 Monmouth County, New Jersey

Joan Reevey, born 1927 Monmouth County, New Jersey

Nellie Reevey, born 1928 Monmouth County New Jersey

Donald Reevey, born 1930 Monmouth County New Jersey

Hosea Reevey, born 1932 Monmouth County New Jersey

Irene Reevey, born 1933 Monmouth County New Jersey

Other Branches of the Revey Family Tree

ISIAH REVEY

Hosea and Fannie (Archer) Reevey's children were (continued)

Margaret Reevey, born Monmouth County, New Jersey

Bertha Reevey, born Monmouth County New Jersey

Georgianna Reevey born 1940 Monmouth County, New Jersey

Lottie Revey was born 1909 in Monmouth County, New Jersey.

Emma Louise Reevey, born 1914 in Monmouth County, New Jersey.

Clarence Reevey was born 1918 in Monmouth County, New Jersey, maybe a sibling.

MARGARET REVEY

Margaret Revey was born on October 11, 1839, in Monmouth County, New Jersey. She was the daughter of Thomas Revey. Margaret Revey married Alfred TAYLOR

EMELINE REVY

Emeline Revy daughter of Isiah and Margaret DWIGHT Revey married George VanBrockle in Monmouth County, New Jersey.

Other Branches of the Revey Family Tree

Brazilla Sinclaire Reevey

Braizilla Sinclaire Reevey, born July 29, 1874, son of Robert and Ann HOLMES Reevey. Barzilla was a farmer and lived in Fair Haven when he registered for the Draft on September 12, 1918. Brazilla wife, Emma Louisa Steward, daughter of Phillip and Caroline (LAWRENCE) Steward

Brazilla and Emma Louis (Steward) Reevey child:

Child: **Dorothy C. Reevey**

Robert Reevey and Ann

George Reevey born 1867

Robert Reevey born 1871

Edmund Reevey born 1872

Brazilla Sinclaire Reevey born 1874

Howard Reevey born 1878

Leon H. Reevey born 1880

Other Branches of the Revey Family Tree

ASA CRUMMEL

Asa Crummel, born 1844, in Monmouth County, New Jersey. Asa Crummell married **Emma Richardson**, and lived in Ocean Township, New Jersey.

Asa and Emma (Richardson) Crummel's children were

Elias Crummel,

Rudolph Crummel,

Ryas Crummel.

The Crummel family lived in Fair Haven, Upper Freehold, and Burlington, New Jersey.

In 1905, Asa Crummel, 49, Hester O. Crummel, 45, and William Crummel lived in Burlington, New Jersey. Asa stated, he was born in Indian Mills, New Jersey. Indian Mills is a history place for Native Americans.

Revey Family Marriages

REVEY FAMILY MARRIAGES

REVEY FAMILY	SPOUSE	DATE OF MARRIAGE	PLACE OF MARRIAGE	JUSTICE OF THE PEACE/ REVEREND
Abby Revey	James H. Reed	December 11, 1893	Monmouth County, NJ	
Abigail Revy	Samuel Dwight	October 15, 1798	Monmouth County, NJ	T. Little
Abigail Revey	Samuel Dwight	December 16, 1826	Monmouth County, NJ	J. Barclay
Abigail Revey	Edward Berry	March 10, 1810	Monmouth County, NJ	
Andrina Revey	Louis Livingston	1881	Eatontown, NJ	
Benjamin Revey	Cathherine Runyon	December 7, 1805	Middlesex County, NJ	
Benjamin Revey	Mary Ann Revey	April 22, 1830	Shrewsbury, NJ	J. Williams
Benjamin Revey	Mary Elise Nickens	November 28, 1867	Eatontown, NJ	T. Wilson
Benjamin Revey	Lenora Brown	April 29, 1891	FairHaven, NJ	
Benjamin Revy	Wm E. Revey	June 6, 1899	Eatontown, NJ	
Cathrine Revey	John W. Harrison	October (?), 1866	Monmouth County, NJ	G. Rice
Catherine Revey	Joesph Richardson	December 29, 1893	Red Bank, NJ	
Charles Reevey	Charlotte Arnold	March 15, 1858	Freehold, NJ	
Delaphine Revey	Elias Livingston	March 23, 1898	Red Bank, NJ	

Revey Family	Spouse	Date of Marriage	Place of Marriage	Justice of the Peace/Reverend
Emeline Revy	William Richardson	February 24, 1820	Monmouth County, NJ	J. Williams
Isiah Revy	Margaret Dwight	September 23, 1823	Monmouth County,NJ	J.Wooley
Lillian Revey	Henry J. Polhemus	January 22, 1898	Eatontown, NJ	
John Revy	Catherine Richardson	October 21, 1864	Monmouth County, NJ	T. Wilson
Jerushy Revey	Samuel Richardson	September 5, 1829	Monmouth County, NJ	J. Barclay
Margaret A. Reavey	Albert J. Bearey	November 22, 1871	Shrewsbury, NJ	
Mary Revey	Aaron Lee	June 1, 1827	Shrewsbury, NJ	J. Barclay
May Rivey	Thomas Moyes	March 26, 1879	Ocean Town, NJ	
Robert Revey	Sarah Richardson	July 9, 1836	Monmouth County, NJ	L. White
Robert Revey	Anne Holmes	Unknown	Monmouth County, NJ	
Samuel Revey	Mary Adams	June 30, 1872	Oceanville, NJ	T. Cook
Sharlotte Reavey	Theodore Johnson	February 11, 1840	Red Bank, NJ	
Silas Reve	Alice Wilkins	April 28, 1746	Monmouth County, NJ	
Thomas Revy	Margaret Revy	November 16, 1800	Shrewsbury, NJ	T. Little
William H. Revey	Francis Demond	September 10, 1883	Fair haven, NJ	
William (Rury)Revy	Diannah Booth	November 15, 1812	Monmouth County,NJ	

Sand Hill Indians

Of

Monmouth County, New Jersey

Sand Hill Indians of Monmouth County, New Jersey

The Revey family relate to the Sand Hill Indians of Monmouth County, New Jersey. James "Lone Bear" Revey, the son of Robert and Mary Revey, was dedicated to preserving the indigenous ancestry of the Revey family.

Plate 55. Tribal council of the Sand Hill band of Delaware, New Jersey, in native costume. The man in the center is Chief Crummel. The man at viewer's extreme left is Robert Revey, father of James Revey. The two men second from either end are wearing the traditional feather crown or "turkey hat" and Chief Crummel is wearing his bald eagle headdress and carrying his bald eagle fan. Photograph taken in the 1920's. Photo courtesy of James Revey.

New Jersey is our homeland. Our ancestors are buried here. We fought to retain our land and lost to the Europeans. We were placed on a reservation, the only one ever in the State of New Jersey. Despite all this, our people remain strong and vibrant, and our tribal government is still intact.

TRIBAL FAMILIES BY COUNTY AND NAME

Delaware/Lenape		Keetoowah/Cherokee	
County	Family Name	County	Family Name
Morris	Clay Hill Ray Thompson	Passaic & Sussex	Davis Holloway Myer Wolfe
Monmouth & Burlington	Clay Ray Reevey Thompson Van Etta	Monmouth & Burlington	Crummel Davis Holloway Horner Richardson Myer Waters

This information was compiled by Lone Bear Revey in 1973 under the auspices of the New Jersey Indian Office.

New Jersey Tribes

Cherokee Nation of New Jersey

182 Ellery Ave

Newark, NJ 07106

(973) 489-1368

C.W. Longbow, Principal Chief

Nanticoke Lenni –Lenape Indians of New Jersey

State Recognized *

POB 544

18 East Commerce Street

Bridgeton, NJ 08302

(609) 455-6910

Fax: (609) 455-5338

Sand Hill Band of Indians

Carroll Medicine Crow Holloway, Principle Chief

POB 1012

Montague, NJ 07827

(732) 455-9055

Powhatan Renape Nation

State Recognized*

Rankokus Indian Reservation

POB 225

Rancocas, NJ 08073

(609) 261.4747

Fax: (609) 261.7313

Ramapough Lenape Nation

State Recognized*

189 Stag Hill Road

Mahwah, NJ 07430

(201) 529. 1171

Fax: (201) 529.3212

Taino Jatibonuc Tribe of Puerto Rico

703 South Eighth Street

Vinland, NJ 08360

REVEY FAMILY SEARCH INDEX

REVEY FAMILY SEARCH INDEX

Within the pages of the Revey Family Search Index lies a comprehensive summary, a crucial compendium of vital information that serves as a compass for those on the journey to connect their individual branch to the expansive and intricate Revey family tree. This meticulously curated index is designed to empower and guide genealogists and family historians in their pursuit of understanding and mapping their familial roots. Embedded within its entries are key details, essential for weaving together the rich tapestry of the Revey family's history.

At the core of the Revey Family Search Index are the foundational elements that anchor each entry: the name, birth date, and the crucial links to parents and spouses. These pivotal details lay the groundwork for establishing connections and tracing lineages, providing a roadmap for individuals eager to unravel the stories embedded within their family history.

Names are not merely labels; they are conduits through time, carrying the weight of familial legacies and histories. The Revey Family Search Index captures the essence of everyone, immortalizing their presence within the broader familial narrative. A name serves as an entry point into the labyrinth of the past, unlocking doors to the stories of those who came before, and those who will follow.

Birth dates, like celestial markers, pinpoint moments in time that shape the trajectory of individual lives. The inclusion of this temporal dimension in the Revey Family Search Index is a deliberate choice, recognizing the significance of birth dates in tracing familial connections and understanding the context of an individual's place within the family chronicle.

Parental connections are the threads that bind generations together. The Revey Family Search Index meticulously documents these ties, acknowledging the role of parents in shaping the familial tapestry. Understanding the lineage from which one emerges provides not only a sense of belonging but also a deeper appreciation for the interwoven stories that collectively form the Revey family narrative.

Spouses, too, play a pivotal role in the family saga. The inclusion of their names, with the maiden's name thoughtfully recorded, adds a layer of complexity and depth to the Revey Family Search Index. It acknowledges the fusion of two lineages, celebrating the union of families and the creation of new branches in the ever-expanding family tree.

The Revey Family Search Index is not merely a compilation of data; it is a living document that invites exploration and sparks the imagination. Behind each entry lies a unique story waiting to be uncovered, a narrative that extends beyond the confines of names and dates. It beckons to genealogists, encouraging them to delve deeper, to ask questions, and to unearth the hidden gems of familial history.

As individuals embark on their journey through the Revey Family Search Index, they are equipped with a valuable tool that transcends the limitations of time. This index serves as a bridge between past and present, offering a tangible connection to ancestors who once walked the same earthly paths. It is a testament to the enduring nature of family bonds, where the echoes of the past resonate in the lived experiences of descendants.

Genealogical research often involves navigating through the labyrinth of historical records, where gaps and ambiguities can obscure the path to understanding one's roots. The Revey Family Search Index, with its clarity and conciseness, serves as a beacon in this labyrinth, guiding researchers through the maze of information and providing a solid foundation for further exploration.

In the quest to connect with the Revey family tree, the Revey Family Search Index stands as a cornerstone, offering a starting point for genealogists to trace their lineage and discover the stories that define their familial identity. Its structured format ensures that vital information is readily accessible, empowering researchers to build a more comprehensive picture of their ancestry.

The Revey Family Search Index is not a static entity; it is a dynamic resource that evolves as new information comes to light. Genealogical research is an ongoing journey, and the index is a living testament to the commitment to uncovering the past. As researchers contribute their findings and share their discoveries, the Revey Family Search Index becomes an ever-expanding repository of knowledge, fostering collaboration and a collective effort to piece together the intricate puzzle of the Revey family's history.

In the pages of a genealogy book, the Revey Family Search Index takes on a special significance. It is a chapter within the larger narrative, a guide that beckons to those with a thirst for understanding their roots. Each entry is a portal to a bygone era, inviting readers to traverse the corridors of time and connect with the individuals who laid the foundation for the present generation.

As the Revey Family Search Index finds its place in the annals of genealogy, it becomes a legacy. It is a gift to future generations, a roadmap that enables them to traverse the familial landscape and discover the stories that have shaped their identity. In the tapestry of genealogical exploration, the Revey Family Search Index is a thread that weaves together the diverse branches of the Revey family tree, ensuring that the stories of ancestors endure and resonate across time.

REVEY FAMILY SEARCH INDEX

NAME	DATE OF BIRTH	PARENTS	SPOUSE
Reevy (male)	Oct. 14, 1879	Charles Reevy Taylor	
Reevy (male)	Apr. 29, 1897	Willaim Reevy Leonora Brown	
Reevy, (male)	Apr. 17, 1887	William Reevy Serena Demond	
Revey, (female)	Feb 18, 1889	Williametta Revey	
Abigail Revy	About 1780		Dwight Berry Aron Lee
Ada L. Revey	1909	Charles Revey Harriett	James Hughes
Abigail Revey	1842	Richard Revey Nancy	

REVEY FAMILY SEARCH INDEX

NAME	DATE OF BIRTH	PARENTS	SPOUSE
Alberta Reevey	1902	John Reevey Sarah Coy	
Alonzo Revey	1880	Charles Reevey Mary Taylor	Justien
Amos Henry Revy	Sep. 1901	Richard Revey Esther Vincent Rebecca E.	Esther Mablen
Andrina Revey	1867	Benjamin Revey Mary Elise Nickens	Louis Livingston Sep. 1885
Augustine Revy	1866	Ebenezer Revy Ann Holmes	Ann Lise
Benjamin Reevey	1805	Benjamin Revey Catherine Runyon	Mary Ann Revy

REVEY FAMILY SEARCH INDEX

NAME	DATE OF BIRTH	PARENTS	SPOUSE
Beatrice Revy	Jan. 1914	Richard Revey Esther Vincent	
Benjamin Revey	Abt. 1780	Unknown	Catherine Runyon Dec. 7, 1805 Middlesex, NJ
Benjamin Revey	1835	Richard Revey Nancy	Mary Elise Nickens
Benjamin C. Revey	1876	William R. Revey	Sarah
Benjamin C. Revey	1871		Lenora Brown
Blanche E. Reevey	Dec 1896	Richard P. Reevey Rebecca E. Holmes	

REVEY FAMILY SEARCH INDEX

NAME	DATE OF BIRTH	PARENTS	SPOUSE
Bloomfield Revey		Benjamin Revey Mary. E. Nickens	1. Fannie VanBrockle 2. Georgianna Thornton
Brazilla Revey	1878	Robert Revey Anna Holmes	
Carina Reevey	1911	Samuel Reevey Carrie	
Catherine Revey		Benjamin Revey Mary E. Nickens	John Richardson
Catherine Reevey	1844	Benjamin Reevey Mary Ann Revy	

REVEY FAMILY SEARCH INDEX

NAME	DATE OF BIRTH	PARENTS	SPOUSE
Catherine Revey	1872	William R. Revey	George Armstrong
Charles Reavey	1847	Benjamin Reevey	Hagar A.
Charles Benjamin Revey			
Charles Edward Revy	Jan. 14, 1876	Charles Reevey Mary A. Taylor	Harriett Lavina
Charles Revey	1851	Richard Revey Nancy	
Charles S. Reevey		Benjamin Reevey Mary A. Revy	
Charlotte Reevey	1887	Thomas Reevey Lavina Thompson	Mr. King

REVEY FAMILY SEARCH INDEX

NAME	DATE OF BIRTH	PARENTS	SPOUSE
Clarence Revey	1919	Benjamin C. Revey Sarah L.	
Cordelia Reevey		Charles E. Reevey Mary A. Taylor	
David Revey		Isiah Revey Margaret	Nellie
Deborah Revy	1857	Isiah Revy	
Ebenezer Revey	1847	Thomas Revey Isabel	Ann Holmes
Ebenezer Franklin Revey	1877	Ebenezer Reevey Ann Holmes	Isabelle
Edward Revey	1912	Augustine Reevey Dora Williams	

REVEY FAMILY SEARCH INDEX

NAME	DATE OF BIRTH	PARENTS	SPOUSE
Edward Revey	1872	Robert Revey Ann Holmes	
Elizabeth Susan Revey	1826	Richard Peter Revey Susan VanSneaden	Issac Richarddson
Ethel Revey	1894		
Emeline Revey	1850	Isiah Revey Margaret Dwight	George Vanbrockle
Emma Reevy	Nov 1910	Samuel H. Reevy Lottie C.	
Estella Reevey		Charles E. Reevey Mary A. Taylor	
Esther Revey		Richard Revey Esther Vincent	

NAME	DATE OF BIRTH	PARENTS	SPOUSE
Eugene Reevey		Charles E. Reevey Mary A. Taylor	
Eva Reevey		William R. Revey	George Polhemus Oct. 17, 1893
Florence Reevey	1889	Thomas D. Reevey Lavina Thompson	Mr. Williams
Frances Reevey	1914	Augustine Reevey Dora Williams	
Frank Revey			

REVEY FAMILY SEARCH INDEX

NAME	DATE OF BIRTH	PARENTS	SPOUSE
Gertrude Reevey	1924	Augustine Reevey Dora Williams	
George Reevey		Isaiah Revey Margaret Dwight	
Harold Reevey	1910	Augustine Reevey Dora Williams	
Herbert Reevey	1913		
Harriett Reevey	1828	Benjamin Reevey Mary Ann Revy	
Henry Revey			

REVEY FAMILY SEARCH INDEX

NAME	DATE OF BIRTH	PARENTS	SPOUSE
Hosea Reevy	Aug 1898	Samuel H. Reevey Lottie C.	Fannie Archer
Howard Reevey		Robert Reevey Anna	
Ida Reevey	1903	John Reevey Sarah Coy	
Isabelle Reevey	1880	Thomas D. Reevey Lavina Thompson	
Isaac Revy	1824		Margaret Dwight
James Revy	1819	Benjamin Revey Catherine Runyon	

REVEY FAMILY SEARCH INDEX

NAME	DATE OF BIRTH	PARENTS	SPOUSE
James R. Revey	1895	Johnson Benjamin Revey Restella Richardson	
Jane Revey	1866	Isiah Revy Margaret Dwight	
John Reevey		John Reevey Sarah Coy	
Joseph Revey	1818	Benjamin Revey Catherine Runyon	
Joseph Revey	1833	Benjamin Reevey Mary Ann Revy	
Joseph Revey	1856	Richard Revey Nancy	
NAME	**DATE OF BIRTH**	**PARENTS**	**SPOUSE**
Joseph	1907	Samuel Revey	

Revey		Carrie	
Kingdom Reevey	1915	Charles E. Reevey Harriett	
Laura V. Reevey	1893	Thomas D. Revey Lavina Thompson	Mr. Johnson
LeGrant Revey	1888		

REVEY FAMILY SEARCH INDEX

NAME	DATE OF BIRTH	PARENTS	SPOUSE
Leona Revy	Oct 1905	Richard Revy Esther Vincent	
Leon H. Revey	1880	Robert Revey Ann	
Leroy Reevey	1905	John Reevey Sarah Coy	Lulu Brewington
Lester Revey	1920	Ralph Revey Louise	
Lewis Revy	1863	Isah Revy Margaret Dwight	
Lottie C. Reevy	Jan 1901	Samuel H. Reevy Lottie C.	
Lucinda Revy		Isiah Revy Margaret Dwight	

REVEY FAMILY SEARCH INDEX

NAME	DATE OF BIRTH	PARENTS	SPOUSE
Nelson Revy	1878	Richard Revey Rebecca E. Holmes	
Madeline Revy	May 1910	Richard Revy Esther Vincent	
Margaret Reevey	1841	Benjamin Reevey Mary Ann Revy	
Margaret Revey	1846	Richard Revey Nancy	
Martha Revey	1898		
Mary Ann Revy	Abt. 1810	Joseph Revy Harriett	Benjamin Reevey Apr. 22, 1830

REVEY FAMILY SEARCH INDEX

NAME	DATE OF BIRTH	PARENTS	SPOUSE
Mary E. Reevey	1882`	Thomas D. Reevey Lavina Thompson	
Mary Revey	1838	Richard Revey Nancy	
Meenao Reevey	1907	John Reevey Sarah Coy	
Norman Reevey	Mar 1894	Samuel H. Reevey Lottie C.	
Olivia Reevey	1920	Charles E. Reevey Harriett	William H. Quill
Orlean Revey		Issac Revey Margaret Dwight	
Oscar Revy	1871	Ebenezer Revy Ann Holmes	

REVEY FAMILY SEARCH INDEX

NAME	DATE OF BIRTH	PARENTS	SPOUSE
Phineas Revey	1869	Benjamin Revey Mary E. Nickens	Margaret Coy
Ralph Revey	1880	Richard Revey Rebecca E. Holmes	
Ralph Henry Revey	Mar 6, 1921	Augustine Reevey Dora Williams	Beatrice Shields
Rebecca Revey	1800		Richardson
Rebecca Revey	1848	Richard Revey Nancy	
Rosella Reevey	1912	John Reevey Sarah Coy	
Robert V. Revey	1896	Johnson B. Revey Restelle Richardson	

Rosanna Reevey	1831	Benjamin Reevey Mary Ann Revy	
Richard Revey	Abt 1800		Sarah Richardson Jul 9, 1826

REVEY FAMILY SEARCH INDEX

NAME	DATE OF BIRTH	PARENTS	SPOUSE
Richard Revey	1814	Benjamin Revey Catherine Runyon	Nancy (Lydia)
Richard Revey	1850	Benjamin Reevy Mary Ann Revy	
Robert A. Revey	1855		Esther Vincent (Rebecca E.)
Oliver R. Revey	Jul 15, 1897	Robert H. Revey Aleta S. Polhemus	
Robert Revey	1844		

REVEY FAMILY SEARCH INDEX

NAME	DATE OF BIRTH	PARENTS	SPOUSE
Schockley Reevey	Sep 22, 1896	John Reevey Sarah Coy	Margaret Engley
Samauel H. Revey	Aug 1855	Isiah Revee Margaret Dwight	Lottie C.
Samuel Reevey	1875		Carrie
Samuel H. Reevey	Apr 5, 1896	Samuel H. Reevey Lottie C.	
Samuel Reevey	1916	Samuel Reevey Carrie	
Schockley Reevey	1897	John Reevey Sarah Coy	
Serina Revey	1871	William Revey	Charles Richardson

REVEY FAMILY SEARCH INDEX

NAME	DATE OF BIRTH	PARENTS	SPOUSE
Silas Revey			Alice Wilkens Apr 26, 1746
Stanley Reevey	1920	Augustine Reevey Dora Williams	
Susie Reevey	1895	John Reevey Sarah Coy	
Susie Revey	1908	Samuel Revey Carrie	
Thomas Revey	1840	Richard Revey Nancy	
Thomas Revy	Abt 1780		

REVEY FAMILY SEARCH INDEX

NAME	DATE OF BIRTH	PARENTS	SPOUSE
Thomas Revey	1817	Benjamin Reevey Catherine Runyon	
Thomas Revey	1835	Benjamin Reevey Mary Ann Revy	
Thomas Revy	Mar 1904	Richard Revey Esther Vincent	
Thomas D. Reevey	Jan 1861	Thomas Reevey Isabel	Lavina Thompson
Vianer Revey		Richard Revey Nancy	
Violet Reevey	1918	Charles Reevey Harriett	

REVEY FAMILY SEARCH INDEX

NAME	DATE OF BIRTH	PARENTS	SPOUSE
Warren Revey	1917	Ralph Revey Louise	
Westley Revey	1934	Augustine Revey Dora Williams	
William Revey	1846	Benjamin Revey Mary Ann Revy	
Wiliam Revey	Nov 16, 1851	William Revey	
William Reevey	1850	Thomas D. Reevey Lavina Thompson	

FAMILY JOURNAL

Welcome to the Revey Family Journal, a sacred space within these pages where you are invited to inscribe the unique chapters of your personal family history. This journal serves as a canvas for you to artistically capture and chronicle the branches of your Revey family tree, weaving together the tales that define your familial legacy.

This journal is more than a mere collection of blank pages; it is an intimate repository for your thoughts, reflections, and the narrative threads that connect you to the rich tapestry of the Revey family's past. With each stroke of the pen, you have the power to shape and illuminate the stories that have shaped your identity, contributing to the ongoing saga of the Revey family.

At the heart of the Revey Family Journal is an invitation to explore the depths of your familial roots. Here, you are encouraged to delve into the names, birth dates, and familial ties that bind generations together. As you trace your ancestry, consider the significance of each detail, for within them lie the echoes of those who came before, paving the way for your own unique journey.

The Revey Family Journal recognizes the importance of preserving not only names and dates but also the essence of individuals who populate your family tree. Beyond the skeletal structure of genealogy, this journal is a canvas for the vibrant hues of personal stories. Take the opportunity to document the anecdotes, traditions, and cherished memories that breathe life into the names on your family tree.

As you embark on this personal genealogical journey, consider the profound impact of birth dates as temporal markers. They signify the moments when individuals entered the world, influencing the course of your family's history. Use these pages to reflect on the significance of these dates and to appreciate the interconnectedness of your family's chronicle.

Parental connections, meticulously recorded within this journal, serve as the threads that weave the narrative fabric of your family tree. Acknowledge and celebrate the role of parents in shaping your lineage, recognizing the contributions of those who paved the way for your existence. Through this exploration, you gain a deeper sense of belonging and an appreciation for the intergenerational stories that make up your familial heritage.

Spouses, too, play an integral role in the narrative of the Revey family. As you document their names, including the maiden names of spouses, you contribute to the celebration of unions that created new branches in the family tree. These entries recognize the interconnectedness of families, highlighting the shared histories that converge and diverge through marriage.

The Revey Family Journal is a dynamic vessel for your evolving family story. It transcends the limitations of time, serving as a bridge between past and present. Each entry becomes a tangible connection to ancestors who once walked the same earthly paths, ensuring that their stories endure in the lived experiences of their descendants.

Genealogy is often a journey through the labyrinth of historical records, where gaps and uncertainties may obscure the path to understanding one's roots. The Revey Family Journal, with its blank pages awaiting your narratives, serves as a guiding light in this labyrinth. It encourages you to explore, to ask questions, and to uncover the hidden gems within your family's history.

This journal is not a static repository but a living testament to your commitment to unraveling the past. As you contribute your findings, share your discoveries, and add layers to the Revey Family Journal, it becomes an ever-expanding treasure trove of familial knowledge. Your entries join a chorus of voices, forming a collective effort to piece together the intricate puzzle of the Revey family's history.

Within the context of a genealogy book, the Revey Family Journal holds a special place. It is a chapter within the larger narrative, a personal account that adds depth and nuance to the collective story of the Revey family. Each blank page is an invitation to traverse the corridors of time, connecting with the individuals who shaped the foundation for the present generation.

As the Revey Family Journal finds its place within the annals of genealogy, it transforms into a legacy. It is a gift to future generations, a roadmap for them to traverse the familial landscape and discover the stories that have shaped their identity. In the tapestry of genealogical exploration, the Revey Family Journal is a thread that weaves together the diverse branches of the Revey family tree, ensuring that the stories of ancestors endure and resonate across time.

FAMILY JOURNAL

FAMILY JOURNAL

FAMILY JOURNAL

FAMILY JOURNAL

FAMILY JOURNAL

FAMILY JOURNAL

FAMILY JOURNAL

FAMILY JOURNAL

FAMILY JOURNAL

FAMILY JOURNAL

FAMILY JOURNAL

FAMILY JOURNAL

FAMILY JOURNAL

FAMILY JOURNAL

FAMILY JOURNAL

FAMILY JOURNAL

FAMILY JOURNAL

FAMILY JOURNAL

FAMILY JOURNAL

FAMILY JOURNAL

FAMILY JOURNAL

About the Author

Dr. Guadalupe Vanderhorst Rodríguez is not just a skilled genealogist; she is the living embodiment of a family's rich tapestry, with roots tracing back to the esteemed lineage of Benjamin and Mary E. (Nickens) Revey.

Armed with over 40 years of dedicated genealogical research, Dr. Rodríguez has become a beacon for those seeking to illuminate the shadows of their own family histories.

Her journey into the world of genealogy began as a volumeter at the Family History Center in Plattsburgh, New York, a role that saw her diligently assisting others in uncovering the hidden gems within their family trees. Driven by an insatiable curiosity and a passion for unraveling the intricate threads of the past, she immersed herself in the study of U.S. Census data, birth, marriage, and death records, becoming a maestro in deciphering the cryptic script of old English handwriting and immigration documents.

Dr. Rodríguez's expertise extends beyond the quiet corners of genealogical archives. Her profound understanding of family history, particularly in Clinton County, New York, earned her a well-deserved spotlight on the television program "Who Do You Think You Are." The program showcased her unparalleled ability to piece together the puzzle of ancestral stories, bringing to life the narratives that were once buried in the sands of time.

However, Dr. Rodríguez's intellectual pursuits are not confined to the realm of genealogy alone. She holds a Bachelor of Science degree in Human Services from SUNY Plattsburgh, a testament to her commitment to understanding the intricacies of human relationships and social dynamics. Furthermore, she has delved into the field of alternative medicine, earning a Master of Science in Acupuncture from the New York College of Health Professions. Her academic journey culminated in the achievement of a Doctorate of Acupuncture from the prestigious Pacific College of Health and Sciences.

In her writing, Dr. Rodríguez seamlessly weaves together the analytical precision of a genealogist with the holistic perspective of a healthcare professional. Her narratives are not just about names and dates; they are tapestries of human experiences, filled with the triumphs and tribulations of generations past.

Whether she is guiding individuals through the labyrinth of their ancestry or exploring the interconnectedness of health and heritage, Dr. Guadalupe Vanderhorst Rodríguez stands as a luminary in the fields of genealogy and holistic health. Her journey, marked by unwavering dedication and a thirst for knowledge, continues to inspire others to embark on their own quests to discover the stories that define them.